Poems

with
themed notes

SAM GRANT

Published by Sam Grant
Publishing partner: Paragon Publishing, Rothersthorpe
First published 2016

© Sam Grant 2016

The rights of Sam Grant to be identified as the author of this work have been asserted by him in accordance with the Copyright, Designs and Patents Act of 1988.
All rights reserved; no part of this publication may be reproduced, stored in a retrieval system, or transmitted in any form or by any means, electronic, mechanical, photocopying, recording or otherwise without the prior written consent of the publisher or a licence permitting copying in the UK issued by the Copyright Licensing Agency Ltd. www.cla.co.uk

ISBN 978-1-78222-464-8

Book design, layout and production management by Into Print
www.intoprint.net
+44 (0)1604 832149
Printed and bound in UK and USA by Lightning Source

FOREWORD

The author's first poem Dispatch Time was published by Allied Press. Seven poems in this collection have been published in previous anthologies.

The sea poem "Eye of the Storm"was short listed in a 2014 competition and subsequently published in an anthology named Poetry Treasures. Sam realized, that a body of work had developed in the process of entering poetry competitions and through ongoing novel and short story writing. Poems, which developed while working towards the completion of a novel. Characters and situations developed from the composing of poems.

The sea poems, which were taken from life experiences assisted Sam, to capture the atmosphere and ship life detail sought in his sea adventure thriller Atlantic Hijack.

Sam Grant's published novels are Atlantic Hijack (2014), a sea thriller adventure story and most recently Dancing on the Beach (2016), a romantic thriller. Pre-views are available on Amazon online. Both novels are now available in a print edition and also on Kindle.

The poems were composed from the year 2000 to March, 2016.

POEMS

Photon Waves 7
Dimensions 8
A Guiding Light 10
"Captured into Their Realm" 11
Cargo to be Stowed (Circa, 1962)* 14
Coming Home (Circa,1962) * 17
Tropical Rain Storm* 20
Eye of the Storm. 23
Cosmic Eye 25
Couch grass meets Dandelion 27
Imaginary Affair 29
In Bed by the Inglenook. 31
That First Liking for Curry 35
Love's True Devotion. 38
Ode to a Clematis. 40
Silent Tongue 42
Forthcoming Royal Birth (Prince George) 44
Memorable Event (1963) * 46
A year gone 51
Dispatch Time 54
Life's River 57
Subliminal Talk 58
Essence of Love Mother Figure 60
Millennium Primrose 62
Holidays past 64
Riding Through Time 68
She left 69
Love Starved by Electronics 71
Spirit of Spring 72
The planted Copse 74
Thankful Thoughts 76
That First Meeting 78

A Shoreline of Love 80
Winter River Race 82
The Three G Summit 84
Poem: About Winter 87
Instant Coffee making..89
The Time Maker's Kingdom 90
Coded in the Wind 93
Ancestral Savannah 95

SIX SEA POEMS*
PHOTON WAVES

Former friends are over there,
dancing in the photon waves, come what may.
Within sun's ray caress on this window sill;
waves that break, turn as they wish.
Many particles, not obeying laws of physics.
when I look, only then, are they there.

Nothing is there but then it is.
We search with clumsy microscope
to seek tangential material.
We see with parallax~ eyes~ movement ~form
—why should they not be there~ even
if we are turned away? They live and breathe
within a fabric that we will never see~
unless sensing inwardly when we turn gulping, gasping, praying
yet with wakened eyes.
There within Planck's theory they sing and
practice dance; entrance there companions over there
in every way~ in new born light.

~~~~~~~~~~~~~~~~

The discovery that photons were both particles and waves has since led to the founding of Quantum physics, and string theory. These discoveries were not only scientifically amazing, but have allowed poets to imagine other worlds, with back up from scientific breakthroughs. With poetry at times a blur, at times, between the boundaries of reality and fantasy.

DIMENSIONS

Separate dimensions,
in unique pattern.
Waves of melodic vibration,
hidden not now discovered.

Strands forever weaving
unique in determination.
Individually defined
from extraordinary mind.

Vibrational strings.
A many latticed web
caught in each realm.
Shut from all our eyes.

Each with intrinsic note,
swirling through a host.
Adjusting to the tempo
materially its own.

Resonating chords,
from each dimension's heart.
Gossamer threads weaving,
frames of individual part.

Myriad particles;
infinitely sparkling;
describing totality,
to all that's held within.

Intimating theories;
that await practical result.
for a break in the mist,
to let us go on through.

String theory scientists conjecture operates in a practical sense, if the strings can vibrate through ten dimensions. More will be understood about minute sub atomic particles, but the artist and poet can weave an interpretation into these extra dimensions. Perhaps we may only be able to paint descriptions from imagination? But then does imagination itself create existence over time? Not just in our lives, but in future direction and understanding of matter? Twenty five per cent of the universe is apparently dark matter. But then perhaps one day we will develop extra-terrestrial eyes that can see these other dimensions or even visit them. More exciting than going to live on Mars, perhaps?

A GUIDING LIGHT

Greet the morning light
that seeks you out
with thankfulness.
Crumpled, dissembled,

stumbling on the
floor of life.
It arrives to rescue you
from phantoms
of the night.
Striking its way thru' clouds
to gaze supreme
on form and colour.

That warms the sea,
turns seed to plant;
breaking darkness
out of sight.
Be in our inner being
Not just in daily meeting,
but in future expanse
let there always be
that guiding light.

~~~~~~~~~~~~~~~~~~~~~~~~~~~~~~~~~

Existence, for some of us, can appear like a discovery made later in the day. There may be people who bound out of bed and see themselves and everything that's before them through a clear prism. Able to feel vibrantly present in the new day. There are those of us who journey back to this appreciation, later in the day. Guiding light is for this category of person.

"CAPTURED INTO THEIR REALM"

'My name we decided is~ Adriana.'
The cold detached look
releasing chill appreciation.
The realization that
alien specie was now
mimicking~ human kind.

They were
in control;
intelligent sources
beyond that of earth.

Raised arms, palms spread, as if
to clasp a waist, then raised again.
Hands turning inwards
downwards, making for
darkness in the waiting room.

My person, being
captured, taken,
away to their reality;
a light then returning
unreal but brighter.
Give for you light.
A pretence for you
That life is as before.'

a light then returning;
We give for you light.
A pretence for you
that life is as before.'

'There is but darkness
beyond that which
we give to you.

No need for light;
'We are no longer
in your domain
we reach like wind 'cross
galactic plains
to instruct, construct
all energy / matter/ force.
In darkness;
our energy supreme.
We give understanding.'

'You are to be attentive
before we place you
back to earth.
Human life~

~is other time.
You are here
~ by invitation.'

'I'll miss my train
if I stay here,'
was what I said.
Silly thing now to say,
to Adriana and
The Galactic command force.

~~~~~~~~~~~

    A poem, which developed after several chapters of novel preparation. The narrative moves forward with James having to become accustomed to the alien presence of this Adriana.
    A poem precis of an early chapter and James's recollection of this encounter. Adriana is an

ambassadorial representative from the Galactic Command Force tasked to recruit the party, who are to colonize Mars. James encounters this entity in Stroud's train station's waiting room. It is the week of the Pagan festival. Encounters with weirdly dressed people are to be expected, but not with extra-terrestrials!

FOUR SEA POEMS
CARGO READY YET? (CIRCA 1962)

Hammer planks on crates,
                         hold them firm in place.
Pin down all lorry chassis,
                         with wire on wheel and ship.
Layer on layer of dunnage;
                         protect cargo from contaminating sweat.
Planks criss-cross lower hold,
                         a'fore railway lines are stacked.
Tin plate boxes of great weight,
                         swing from shore to ship.
Bedded three deep,
                         in first three lower holds.

Clouds of dust form by,
                         five hold, as clay is neatly stacked.
Faces, muffled, grab hold the bags.
                         Get extra pay for dust.
Now a single- decker bus,
                         swings with ropes to guide.
The 'tween decks fill with buses,
                         holds with crated cars.
Boxes of whisky, gin and Drambuie,
                         in a special cargo locker.
Tally taking care,
                         still makes count fall short.

Bags of plastic pellets,
                         for factories far afield,
are skilfully stacked;
                         as space is all but filled.

Are we nearly ready?

Drums of ethanol,

Tugs arrive;

ready to take on ;

No, no, not yet.

need stacking on the deck.

Our cargo work complete

that mistress of the deep.

~~~~~~~~~~~~~~~~~~~~

- Ships were driven by wind and sail. Then the steam engine was adapted to drive paddle wheels and propellers. Engineering and design efficiency meant steam replaced sail. The motor ships, were a later progression from the coal burning steam ships. The motor cargo ship, depicted in "Cargo ready yet," housed an engine below the mid-ships accommodation. The five pillar like pistons, punched up and down to drive the single propeller. A generator, one of three constantly ran to provide heat and light at sea. In port or when hauling aboard the anchor cable a second generator would be started. The electricity generated sufficient to power a small town.

    On deck there were two masts on the foredeck and one on the after deck . Masts a memory from sailing ship days, but now with derrick head blocks attached to the main cross structure with the long tubular lift derricks strapped down at deck level while at sea. The main deck a riveted structure painted red. The five green canvassed cargo hatches, like wedged packages waiting to be opened when the ship reached port. Wooden accommodation decks with pitch melted and trickled between the planks. Another carry forward from the days of sail. A Giro compass kept that close approximation to true north and was the main compass for steering by. The magnetic one, housed in the wheel now a comparison check. These needed first correcting for both deviation and variation to establish an accurate course.

COMING HOME (CIRCA 1962)

Vast tracts of ocean cross'd,
with engine pistons pounding;
Thru' tropical sea and sun,
to turbulent winter water.
Sea and wind subdued;
coast's now in view.
The cables rapid rush,
emits a cloud of rust

Pilot boards, at dawn,
for the going- in.
Ship now's a- turning,
with tugs at bow and stern.

A monkey's fist,
sends line to shore.
Uncoiling ropes give,
out stench of oil and tar.
Sudden engine burst,
stops all forward motion;
brings deck to a tremor;
a- tingling feet, legs, and body.

Rope thrice round
the winch is wrapp'd~slack,
is taken in- til' drum taut- fibre slips and creaks.

Criss- cross wire and rope,
run from ship to quay.
Gangway lowers~ while tarpaulins,
get rolled back, hatches lifted.
Pipes lower'd to the grain mounds;
drawing out the cargo,
like giant drinking straws.

To fill the silo- empty out the holds.
Grain scented heavy air,
taken in by lungs.
A South Atlantic harvest
to feed both man and beast.
The crew now excited,
For the sign off
and this ship in memory.

~~~~~~~~~~~~~~~~

By modern standards an 8,000 ton cargo liner does not sound enormous.

But during the twentieth century it was profitable to run these ships from the United Kingdom to Argentina and back fully loaded. The freight charges levied by the shipping company might pay for the build of a ship after one voyage to South America. Compared with container transport the method of loading, unloading and storing of cargo both complex and time consuming. The question might be asked why were containers not used earlier? But Britain made and exported a vast array of goods. Not all suitable for containerization. Heavy packages of steel plate and locomotives are two examples.

The smaller retail product manufactured in China is ideal for storing and carrying in containers. More finished product was being imported into Britain and there were efficiency savings to be made also in building bulk carriers able to carry iron ore and grain, rather than the smaller quantities carried by general cargo ships, like the one depicted in "Coming Home." And Atlantic Hijack by Sam Grant.

In the poem the ship has been away for nearly three months. The return voyage back could take over three weeks. A journey from summer to winter. Through the tropics and finally meeting the cold of the North Atlantic. A liner run, which was repeated over and over. Crews might stay on this run for twenty years or more. The crew would pay off and go on leave for two weeks while the cargo was unloaded around the coast. There was excitement at the prospect of shore leave for most. The poem captures the activity associated with port arrival. The arrival procedures like a talisman mark the event.

A TROPICAL RAIN STORM

Clouds reach down
and all but lick the sea;
then the rain slakes
across decks;
caught in what breeze remains.

A hissing, punching on the
metal hatches,
releases steam~ like off the
back of some overheated beast.
Water tumbles furiously
from corrugated awning.
Placed to give shelter
from the fiercest heat.

There is no sun
to sight its Azimuth
for the run today.

It will reach its zenith;
dip and lower
before the clouds disperse
and call cut;
on the blistering, drenching,
pummelling spikes of water flow.
We have no GPS
and now must wait
to catch sight of
stars, moon, planets;
then to capture where we are;
a thousand miles
from nearest land;

A small dot on the space
of this vast Atlantic Ocean.

~~~~~~~~~~~~~~~~~~~~~~~~

    Clouds can sweep into tropical latitudes with the cold temperate waters of the North and South Atlantic meeting up with the perpetually heated tropical waters. The breeze often stilled by a tropical rain storm, which could be over in ten minutes. On the bridge of the ship there most likely would be the Second and Third Mate- maybe the two deck apprentices and even the Captain waiting to spot the sun dance out from behind a swirl of cloud. On cloudy days the sun would often oblige by showing a watery disc to the observer, who looked for the sun's disc through the coloured lens of a sextant. The exact time calculated by Almanac as to when the sun would be vertically overhead, before it would dip on its journey back to sink into the sea at eventide.

    The azimuth obtained would then give a latitude reading and combined with a trigonometric calculation called The Day's Run - with logarithmic valuations obtained from Nories Tables could establish the ship's position at Midday. An accurate measurement of the sea miles travelled by the ship in twenty four hours was needed. A bronze propeller type instrument(the log) twirled in the sea attached to a stout log line- usually from the bridge down to the sea. The dial would register the nautical miles run since the previous days sun-sight. About 130 miles could be the distance run. There was also a calibrated underwater measuring device on cargo liners of the nineteen sixties vintage. A useful check on the logline- but prone to inaccuracy, as I recall. The log dial reading was usually given more credence.

A severe storm could envelope the ship and hide the sun completely. In the poem the storm interrupts the midday azimuth sought to obtain a position. The sun's altitude is obtained in the early morning, which enables a calculation to be made to run forward to midday. Without the midday sun position the accuracy of the position is then downgraded to an estimated position.

In that early evening the First or Third Mate would look to obtain a star sight, while the horizon was still visible as the sun dipped below the horizon. But it would be the Second Mate, as the navigator who would want a position from the star sight as the sun rose next day, to assure that his ship's position calculations were accurate.

From a six star sight, neatly intersecting on the chart he would expect to obtain a position accurate to within a quarter of a mile. Where the ship was found to be away from the course line, the Second Mate would most likely make a course alteration~ to regain the trajectory course pencilled on the chart.

A further sun sight next day would hope to find the ship back on this course. The ship's captain would be looking to see that his ship was on the prescribed course or very close. The shipping company then messaged the ship's position by radio signal. The Second Mate's expertize in the skills of celestial navigation invariably held sway over other bridge participants. Not all were necessarily as accurate. The alteration made on the twelve to four watch by the Second Mate might only be one degree, but could be sufficient to entice the ship back on to its course line.

EYE OF THE STORM

Gripped in Neptune's pitchfork
Held in blocks of rushing green
Tipped skywards, but to plunge
Pancake pounding down
Waves spout thro' railings;
Foams on decks and hatches
Then waterfalls right back.
Wind snatching tops of waves
Rips out stinging, spitting spray
~from this there is no rest.

Yet clouds form a pact~pitch black.
A parcel of water opens up
In a tamer world within
Clouds in that domain
deliver sheeted rain;
that spikes the water;
mists the deck
flattens out the sea;
~ all devilish howls without.

A tiny cave of water that in we'll hide;
in this calm small eye
before we exit that other side.
Meet sea river mountains.
Their screaming mistress, banshee cries, and ship waves—higher and higher.

~~~~~~~~~~

Mountainous waves and screaming wind can be terrifying when viewed from the shore, let alone on board a ship. A storm at sea tests both ship and crew. The North Atlantic can produce wave blocks of forty feet streaming toward the ship. The pitch and pounding of the bow leads you to pray that, somehow the ship will manage to pop up again after each successive heavy wave encounter. Columns of sea green spurt through railings and wash over the foredeck. Spray lashes up to the bridge window area. The barometer reading on the bridge is way down. The storm centre can be this calm eerie area of water. The ship will eventually break through the storm, you pray, and into safer, calmer southern waters.

National Poetry competition-2014- Short listed from 6,000 entrants. Published in Poetry Treasures by Forward Poetry.

COSMIC EYE

The Moon above, like one giant eye;
pouting toward the sun.

Are you steward for one, who stands
back upon the cosmic sand?

Do you survey and tell all
to those in other realms?

Are you penetrating with an especial eye
to record man's passage here on Earth?

A sentinel messaging perhaps
all that happens—out across bands of space.

Of races who ruled, scavenged here;
then retraced to realms,
more plentiful than earth.

Leaving this cosmic being;
to pick, record, send, reveal;
all that ever happens here.

Does their imprint run
in our blood,
replenishing, altering
what we think we know?

This satellite moon
Performing harmonic dance;
round land and sea;
collating, replaying
each and every moment.

Oblivious to this are we
for these are not our eyes
ears, voice;

" Will you re-visit
this earth?"
if your cosmic eye
reveals
that man's despoiling
strips away life and beauty.

We~ then not alone,
but being viewed, reviewed;
watched, studied by
advanced specie~
that plays sweet music
to earth moon momentum.

~~~~~~~~~~~~~~~~~~~~~~~~~

    The properties of silicone. The possibilities of rock to store information led to the writing of this poem. Since the poems composition in 2000 the possibility of the moon having extra-ordinary properties has become more plausible. A recent report in 2016 stated that astronauts on the far side of the moon heard sounds that they described as like music.

    This information was stored away from the public view, but its revelation makes for interesting reading. Practical physical application is required to prove theory, but there are exciting possibilities that memory could be stored in material other than by man-made electronic storing technique. It would be both interesting and exciting were a four hundred year old oak tree be able to play back earlier times and depict generations that walked in the forest to admire the oak's its summer foliage, for example.

COUCH GRASS MEETS DANDELION

The couch grass reached
out of the fronds from the fern;
safe it thought, from its former home;
no longer tangled in turf- in a field;
To be poisoned or wrenched out by hand.

'Are you holidaying?'
Asked the dandelion clock,
which chanced to spin
and float on the bank—
midst the fern.

'How dare you speak
of holidaying to me.
I'm in revolution
over discrimination—
as you should be too!'
said the couch grass in utter disgust.

'Why so, asked the dandelion?'
Unaccustomed to harsh word;
I find this bank
an ideal perch
to gaze all day at the sweet sun.

' Have you not heard?'
They're disparaging our birth;
practising genocide;
poisoning the earth
and cursing our worth,'
said the grass now in despair.

'They use derogatory terms.
Like weed~foul pest
Then poison our food.
How do you not know these things?'
~You who floats through the air
And sees their foul practice.

The dandelion's spinning
Clock span away to
A quieter spot
Out of hearing of the
couch grasses war-like talk.

A new golden crown.
soon delighted the bees,
which allowed the
dandelion to spawn
and fly free.
away from strife.

~~~~~~

The fable has had appeal for centuries as a means of describing moral truths. There has been an awakening to the dangers of pesticide and the banned use of DDT is an early example of necessary action.

IMAGINARY AFFAIR

A smile, a look, that conveys some appreciation, for feelings
Trapped, ~~ hoping to be freed by eyes that share
understanding.
Not that altogether, exclusively ~ alone am I aware of
beauty in Lara's body, movement, turn of head, sound of voice.
Snatched from the trivial day to day by movement of thoughts, that
soak the mind. Playing intensely on all matter, meaning,
molecular, physical. The jumping synapses that emit rainbow
colour.
Telling all that persists, exists within the realm of knowing;
That all purpose here on earth is sublimated, prostrated formed
in total
adoration to her exquisiteness of charm, inhabiting~~ taking my
attention from~ all else that ever came, before time—even before
time began.

Yet no progress will be made, because her career she makes,
And me taken like a portmanteau opened, then shut;
when needed for advice or designated for partner pact.
Hijacked to combat a client who wants from Lara something
beyond
a smile. Then I'm hired with flirts and looks to intimate we
itemize.
Like she gives a fig and drops me back, once the signature
on that business contract, is signed and sealed as fact.

Her fragrant scent gets inside me~ but not that
she shows me any signal for hope.
Although I've fallen for her dope.

Nina walked out. I found that so difficult, then that time.
There's never ever been from Lara that move
~~ suggestion, that I might be the one that she could miss!

A love affair never ever starting. Nina's chihuahua
I called a rat, has more chance of making impact.
I just exist like one or other of an adoring pack,
who breathe spell bound in her presence;
waiting for a glance, a smile - even one kind word, perhaps?

~~~~~~~~~~~~~~~~~~

This poem is a reflection by James. (futuristic novel by Sam Grant) His inner thoughts after being ditched by Nina. James originally could not believe his luck that Nina apparently fell for him, but her interest had dimmed. James was beginning to see that it was never going to work. Nina probably had a point in that James was in thrall to Lara. But then so were others! His junior role means the chance of a one to one relationship with Lara is unlikely, but he lives and works in hope. Not that there has been any physical relationship for James with Lara or even the prospect of a date. But Nina obviously wants out. The idea that Lara is getting more attention from him than she is, certainly from a woman's perspective a good reason to leave

IN BED BY THE INGLENOOK

We visited the old lady,
that's Ma and me;
who seemed to be always in bed.
A bed next to an open fire,
that log crackled in winter.

She spoke at length
from that bed.

'The hospital,' she said,
'spoke certain words
did Percy
when they put him under.'

'What words?' asked Ma.
' Swear words,'
said the old lady, giving
out a guttural chuckle;
eyes now sparkling at the thought
of shocking others.

'You'd never expect that
~ so quietly spoken is Percy.'
' Very out of character,'
I told the hospital~
'May be the result of war.'

'One can never tell.'
~ She first paused and said.

Escape came
to that farm garden.
With apples laid in rows
on upstairs barn floor;
musty old books, magazines

broken chairs, old cupboards;
saddles, bridle and reins; brasses,
rosettes, crockery, cutlery and broken
clocks. A treasure trove,
for a child to explore.

Hams hung on hooks
in the parlour,
of that garden.

Judy~ Percy's black and white terrier
jumped over a stick.
Somersaulting, fetching;
standing on two legs.

Back indoors, I remember
the red stain on the waxed wood floor,
~~~That looked~ just like blood!
Who was stabbed just there?
Her husband, I always feared.

'That's dye come out
from the Christmas tree paper.
~ That's all,' she said,
in matter of fact way,
when asked one day.

She was always
In bed, propped
by a pillow.
Full of talk and report
of events near and far.
A supply of Jacob's cream crackers,
on offer, and~~
Soda water that bubbled
up from mouth to nose.

The farm with the wheel.
Water spilling
over the ridges;
moss covered and still.

The crazy paving of the drive.
The neat hedges with
their box tree scent.

That she was always in
that bed by the fire
never troubled
the mind of a child.

With a voice ever strident.
~~ 'Them calves to market
~~next Tuesday,
~~ you're hearing me~ George?'
She would shrilly call out.
Floor tapping her stick,
while lay in that bed.

The manager
Muddy booted now standing
on the grid by the door.

No ordinary bed,
by the inglenook.
More chariot
of war for
this new Boadicea.

~~~~~~~~~~~~~~~~~~

    Straight out of childhood. Mother was from farming
stock. Visits to the farm in Kingskerswell, Devon would

33

have been like going back to the memory of her younger life. Certainly she would have understood the trials and tribulations of the farmer's wife left to run the farm without a husband. Mother's family moved from the Middlesex area, and she was in service, for a time with a family related to the farmer's wife. My father was established as a solicitor at the time of this visit. His family relatives farmed on Exmoor. World War One saw father aged fourteen assisting in guarding a Devon Dartmoor reservoir. It was believed the Germans would attempt to poison them. His father, was a soldier in Egypt. He went in as a private, but ended the war as a Second Lieutenant. In family history you look for significant turning points. This was probably one for my early family. My great uncle worked for the Post Office and was retired when I was a child. Ultimately I joined Royal Mail and was employed as a postman for thirty years before retirement. The social aspirational wheel turned backwards once more with my arrival into the mix.

THAT FIRST LIKING FOR CURRY

Transferring taste to meaning.
New life, faces, places.
That one meal;
a memory stick to back click;
feelings, hopes, and fears.
Stirred alive in taste sense buds.
A role in the casting.
That individual aroma, flavour,
Now forever unlocks memory
of that time; life scene;
from a particular meal.
People, places, talk~ fitting in.

That you also can be, included
in seafarer culture.
Another formed world, which
you hoped would accept you in.
The town like accommodation structure,
with honey comb of
corridors, cabins, where
metal panels vibrate
from a pounding engine.
The deck beneath
rarely still, save at anchor or in port.

Straggling wires and masts,
and green canvassed hatches~
like fields on a red decked earth.
Absorbing most visible space from above~all
to be caught, encircled,
by ever present sea, which
for months will be both work
and home.

Professions of skill abound, with rings
of gold to note each their worth. Will they stand back, ignore
and not converse or with depth of experience, training,
important position, choose not to talk—
green that you are to these roles — defined by skill, ability,
knowledge, competence and experience.
Will you be accepted in this team?

One football game changed all that.
The dusty dingy warehouse bales of wool
did for goalposts. In tatty jeans, shirts,
scuffed work shoes;
engineers in spattered boiler suits;
deck officers un-messed by engine oil.
Senior engineers and those on deck,
whose boiler suits maintained their white.

Second, fourth, fifth and sixth engineers against
the Second and Third deck officers
—Plus we two apprentices.

A nucleus of group, which without
—the ship would cease to run.
And I but the junior apprentice
with much to learn. Yet decided that day
to be adventurous and eat for later,
a first-time curry.
A fiery meal, to baptise me into this
new world encounter.

~~~~~~~~~~

Significant events are printed in your mind. That of
joining a first ship has to be one for every youngster, who

goes to sea. My family were not seafarers. Pre-sea training did help acclimatize me to this world. The largest ships, that I had seen and boarded were destroyers moored alongside a harbour. These were about 2,000 tons. Sleek and purposely built to minimize visibility.

Cargo ships were about 8,000 tons and had tall masts and derricks, and were to me impressively large. The first cargo liner I visited was an Ellerman Line ship alongside in Liverpool Docks. It was a college visit and we were shown around and then given a meal in the dining saloon. In our fifth term we would shortly apply to join a shipping company. This was a pre-view of a foreign-going company ship— The like of which we were going to live and work aboard in the near future.

Those whose father, uncles, brothers were seafarers probably were not that in awe. I was. The sheer size of, for example, the prop shaft in the tunnel down the engine room. The main engine size breath-taking. The strongly pulsed clatter from the generators, which powered both ship and derricks. These demanded that you look to admire their purpose and presence. The cargo holds were cavernous, dark and deep when you peered down into from deck level. This visit to a working cargo ship left me very impressed. Not a shore based pretend ship, but a working, breathing one where everyone on board would likely meld into the ship routine and fulfil both a crucial and respected role.

LOVE'S TRUE DEVOTION

Love's chattering away,
around a corner, down a lane;
now absent from past attention.
Content to be amused ;
while leaving hearts in turmoil,
others badly bruised.

Entranced by its exploits
of piercing hearts with darts;
dipped in narcotic, doping, emotion.
Love may stay away for years.
Then when least expected,
return with pleasure, pain, potion,
to inoculate, anew.
Destroying all resistance,
with the eyes, face, smile, voice,
of one that's all to you.
But then love decides it best keeps,
its own company and charm.
Extracts its mirth, affection, mesmerizing presence.
To go away and chatter—quite alone.

Can you objectify love? Can you make love into a credible being, that operates with the wiles and subterfuge of a person? The poem is not unlike the song which speaks of that devil called love. The refrain also, which states -I'm never going to fall in love again. The drug like quality of love is there for us to experience. Our existence perhaps depends upon our need to never come off this drug completely—Yet after a heart-break experience we can tell the world and ourselves~ never again! There are broken love matches, which effectively can leave those who have loved devastated and in their hearts unable easily to move forward and form a new loving relationship. To offer up love as an entity and existence where it plays tricks with our emotions and is itself the conductor, orchestrator of all relationship match making. Then it can become perhaps an antidote to the acute disappointment we feel when the person we love ceases to love us. The devil called love.

ODE: TO A CLEMATIS

Clematis~ I wait for you.
    Red berries of the holly tree
Scrunched by passing birds
    after the mistletoe has gone;

while the skies of winter
    maraud my view
I wait for you.
    To break open that
white starred petal that may
    compete with snow.

~ but I wait for you;
    to move forward
spring burst of show.
    You are not tempted
by lengthening days
    to open every bud, but
in gradual stage
    entice the early bee to view.
New growth shoots
    above your forming
crown of white.

The days are cold;
    ~but I wait for you.
To move forward
    spring burst of show.
You are not tempted
    by lengthening days
To open every bud, but
    in gradual stages you
Entice the bee to view.
    New growth shoots

                above your forming
crown of white.

The encouraging
    warmth of spring to bring
An exoticism of scent
    developed in ancient vine
Clasping an Asian landscape
    now entwined with
A new land preparing for
    full flower in spring.

    Symbolic messages. There are many. Not everyone is stirred by pictorial image. Words can have more effect on feelings than pictures. The seasons have an emotional hold. We can never really say that we are in control. Symbolic in our lives some will say, rather than definitive. We cannot be unaware of how nature reacts to more daylight. To sense the opportunity to make blossom and flower. Evolution has made plants attuned to change in air temperature, moisture in the soil. The warming even of the soil. We are quite distant from the natural world in our heated and covered house communes. The Clematis is an exotic plant and to see it flowering is a beautiful visual experience. This is not to decry the inherent beauty of flowers like the daffodil and primrose. The white winter flowering Clematis can often almost totally capture stage presence in January or February, where native blossom is still wrapped up in buds to protect itself from frosts.

SILENT TONGUE

What is there, without sound?
What exists, but that which we understand?
Perhaps there is much more, and yet-
t' would scare us to see, hear,
sense, more with mortal eye, ear .
Yet great affection can exist
for that which warms our being—
with emotion~ saying~ "you"~ are not alone.

The mind which networks~
listens to the ramblings
of individual life experience
rejoicing, while still
reciting, remembered praise, request,
and thanks~ within a silent tongue.
A yearning to be heard
by a renewing consciousness;

when man takes for granted
the everyday in life;
rakes out concern for others
~no part of their plans today.

~ But still they want to know
How? ~that even now
you find a powerful love for other
than the day.

None that can be seen,
but you may still stop, to listen
sense~ 'cross time.
The need to go returning to

words that harken loving
embrace from the provider
of life's fountain.

A tongue silent to others, but
full of word and song,
planting seeds of request, praise and love.
Onward goes the silent tongue
chattering out desires, hopes, dreams
in a metaphor,
epitomised in pastures green.

~~~~~~~~~~~~~~~~~~~~~~~

>There is reference to the 23rd Psalm in the final words of the poem. This psalm is an affirmation of belief and through our lives we can belong to religious groups and yet still feel disengaged at a personal level. This psalm proclaims belief at a personal level. It also attempts to give re-assurance, faith and hope. Each day requires renewal in faith and belief. Words spoken silently in prayer and formed in our minds can seem inadequate, but we do not know for sure.

FORTHCOMING ROYAL BIRTH
(Prince George)

      To live in harmony with all family ties.
Not to be separated from the world around,
but allowed to develop and grow to follow
the path he or she may choose,
which may not be that of royal service
or even privilege and rank.
That personal path that an individual needs
to meet a full and worthwhile life.

      It may not be one of recognition
from the inquisitive world without,
but that of artist, scientist, engineer or poet.
All those who live and breathe from deep
accomplishment . Endeavours
that give glow to the immortal soul within.

      To awaken others from that beating drum,
that before for them has shown no respite
of tension, strife along the path of life.
This to follow from loving parents, who understand
the restrictions that inhabit their own royal life.

> This poem was submitted in a competition, but intends to capture the difficulties and restrictions that accompany birth. In particular to a prince and future king. Most of us do have choices about our daily lives uncircumscribed by having a royal role to play. The fortunate among us can be skilled musicians or artists and follow their chosen passion. In very fortunate circumstances be paid sufficiently to make a living while enjoying following this passion to make music, paint or even write.

A poem, which was selected to be published, together with others with the same theme.

MEMORABLE EVENT, 1963

Puerto Ordaz to New Jersey and Back
The New York arrival
all but unnoticed.
Not the Queen Mary's
glamour and glow; shimmering lights;
bejewelled swan, gliding in.
Like Facebook or Twitter.
The ship to shore radio
crackled out messages
on wavebands,
not meant for our ears.

'That limey old rust bucket's,
your next take in.'
'Got you Chief we're movin' in,'
came back the call from that
sleek pilot cutter.

High powered binoculars
trained on our ship,
could hardly miss
flaked deck corrosion,
though deck roller'd red.
splotched brown spots,
spider weaving rust
weeping from pores
of once glossy paint.

The visit
that early July,
but first of many.

Steam heated coils,

In each tank
maintaining oil fluidity
to run through deck pipes
and away ashore.

Oil temperature checks,
thermometer dipping
tanks kept hot
with fluid thin oil,
Preventing cooling to
Inedible black blancmange

Once emptied-
pressure washing
inside every tank.
Then once loaded
~ to New Jersey
~ then right back.

In November sixty three
winter cold took centre stage.
We returned once more
to meet our
favourite pilot cutter.

The radio stuttered and crackled,
Then-
' You're not going in,
President Kennedy's been shot.

'Abort docking procedure
Anchor where you stand.'
The only orders given.
A megaphone blast to
tell of the news~

~ Met with disbelief.
'Kruschev's been shot as well,'
came back one jokey reply.

It was not believed, but true.
Yellow cabs parked to stop
in Time Square,
that fateful day. All stricken
by their President shot dead.

The pumps slowed,
as usual,
from back pressure,
before the tanks emptied.

Then to Venezuela.
Back again before Xmas tide.
Now Jack's face appeared on
stamps, mugs and memorabilia
remembering that day
of terrible lament.

~~~~~~~~~~~~~~~~~~

> Horribly, like nine eleven~ everyone has memories of where they were when John Kennedy was assassinated. I was seventeen years old and like the many who admire Barack Obama I was hugely impressed by President Kennedy. It was hard to accept what we were told. The ship would probably have docked straightaway, until we received this news. I was wheelman on the bridge and remember the Second Mate picking up on the word "abort". An American use of the word which we were unfamiliar with. The instructions were to abort docking~

and anchor where the ship was. We were abandoned for a day by the piloting authority.

Technical Information:~

After berthing alongside a wooden jetty, in Bayonne two pipes would be attached to the discharge manifolds. I remember the jetty as being wooden, because there was a New York tug strike, on one occasion, and the Master berthed without tugs, unfortunately splintering part of it.

The deck watch, which I was part of worked twelve hours on and twelve off. Invariably the oil discharge rate fell. The four steam pumps were miniature steam engines set in the bowels of the ship. Accessed by ladders going down the well from the deck. Two pump houses. One in front and one abaft the accommodation. The pumps pistons needed oil swabbing at half-hourly intervals. A trip to the pump room was not unwelcome when the temperature was well below zero on deck. However, a two week trip south to Venezuela's Orinoco River meant the pump rooms were places to be avoided. The Mate called it a milk run to and fro from the two countries. He was a seasoned tanker man, and held an Extra Master's certificate, although young. The Extra Master's was rated academically and professionally very highly.

Oil discharge might start at a gallop, but back pressure slowed the pumps until they went from a discharge rate of 250 tons to as low as a 100 or even 20 tons per hour. Back pressure, mentioned in the poem, can be caused by distance. An example, of this is when the oil needs to be sent ashore along a lengthy pipe line.

The oil could, in any event become less viscous on cooling, and harder to pump, apart from distance pressure. Also when topping off a refinery~ tank resistance could build from the weight of oil already inside.

The clickety clank of the pumps would drop to a heavy wheeze like sound, which meant a longer stay in port than the company might have liked. It did enable a number of shore leave trips to New York on a Grey hound bus, plus a visit to the World's Fair. Tankers are infamous for being in and out of refineries like lightening.

~~~Turbine steam pumps were installed on the more modern tankers I served on and 6,000 tons an hour discharge rate could be achieved. Probably very slow by modern standards. Nevertheless the tanker could discharge the oil cargo within ten hours.

A YEAR GONE

The sun throws waves
of light, containing
many particles of
extraordinary swirl
hidden to the human eye.
A decoding of translation,
yet to be discovered.
Formatting each year
determining,
encompassing,
deciding, perhaps how
experience~ memory will be wrought.

Obscuring the seeing of where
life's leading~ 'til we look back
on that year gone by.

The best for us
to live in hope
for dream accomplishment.
Perhaps in matters of the heart.

OR
that a packet of
Californian poppy seed, germinates
to burst in vibrant flow
of yellow, orange~~
making you smile the Summer through.

OR
When finally written~
~ a revised, improved story
transformed to final script.

Etched in the memory
of year past.

From out the internet's blue mist
a message arrived.
Agreed publication
of the final missive.

You no longer sat,
adrift in some small boat, but
clambered out of containment
to unwrap the story landed.

Waves choppy
with rocky outcrops
were met and overcome.
Landfall was made.
The bow embedded~ novel
published and ready.

Live, available,
followed through.
~Timeline met.
That diverse, peoples~ young and old
will read, talk~ write~ about your novel
~~ You need then that hope!

~~~~~~~~~~~~~~~~~~~~~~~~

This poem is perhaps difficult to understand for anyone who has never published a novel. Reports are printed of novels that are written starting at seven at night and are completed by seven next morning! A non- stop flow of words, which produces a complete story. Ruth Rendell spoke of writing for several hours every morning. An undoubted successful production line method by an

52

expert crime author. This suggests the venture is fast and does not require contemplation, re-writing and correcting. A much more lengthy process is perhaps more the typical authors experience. First the preparation to final manuscript can need many re-writes and even cuts to original chapters. Re-writing with new ones. The novel has to be made ready for submission and the author can receive rejection after rejection initially.

A literary agent working on your behalf to secure a publishing contract can cost three hundred pounds a month. There may be the idea in writing groups that your novel will be selected and the literary agent will take a percentage from sales. Already successful authors may manage this. The publishers contract in effect unleashing a torrent of cash to pay for your novel. A main publishing house can spend in excess of fifty thousand pounds if they choose your novel. A first novel struggles to get accepted because there is no track record of sales from the author. Unless the author is already a successful writer,

There are exceptions—Katie Price was one of the early celebrity authors. Main steam publishers quickly realized that a celebrity name could produce volume sales. This novel genre can be be ghost written, but fans are likely to buy. Your authentic written and crafted novel takes hard work~ plus inspiration. Where you receive approval from other authors and publishers that can help to affirm the novel for you the author—Self-publishing is an opportunity and even well known authors are known to self publish.

DISPATCH TIME

A momentary quiet;
But that is all.

Soon doorbells will ring
and great bustle begin

The long floor will be home
to six or more men.

Banter will follow,
as the ritual unfolds.

The front box will be emptied,
again and again.
Letters in great clumps
on table will fall.

Stations of progress,
to forward the mail.
Cancelling the stamps
and sorting like hell.

Bags will be tied,
trains will be met.
Sending out mail
across all the world.

~~~~~~~~~~~~~~~~

Rowland Hill devised the postage stamp and kick started a world letter service. The internet's electronic message has now become a major means for both companies and individuals to communicate. The letter post no longer needed to the extent it once was. Streams of letters were and are directed by postcodes. Phosphor prints enabled an optical recognition system to sort vast streams of letters

in a mechanized sorting office environment was devised. This was a massive transformation —before the internet became a dominant force in communication.
Town postal dispatch offices separated and sorted first and second class letters into letter frames. Bundle tying and labelling wads of letters as a box filed. These to be further sorted into destination drop bag fittings. For example, Northampton, Leicester delivery, Leicester distribution, Devon and Cornwall. More immediate destinations refined. In particular, London broken down into districts. Plus separate drop bags for foreign air mail and surface mail. The packets were hand stamped cancelled and separated into first and second class for hand sorting into the labelled drop bag fitting. Emphasis needs to be placed on the "by hand." The poem aims to capture the momentum required to get the dispatch ready.

This Local Office:
From about five in the evening onwards, breaks in the sorting programme were needed to tie and load bags to go by van to the train station. Inward mail for the next day's delivery was brought back by van from both the station and later on the main city office. There was also a separate van run with letter bags and parcels to the city. Maybe forty bags of parcel and twenty letter bags were brought back for next day delivery. Local letter mail remained in the office and was sorted into the town walks. The term "pressure duty" was given to the work of sorting the mail. This was an overtime duty and speed of sorting could vary. There were premier sorters and others who were slow. The term sorting pressure achieved real meaning in these circumstances. Streams of post came in by vans collecting from about thirty rural offices and sixty five town and rural collection boxes, while the front box

needed to be frequently cleared from about four o'clock onwards. The "final box" from the front counter was timed for seven o'clock. The aim was for the dispatch to leave by van for Leicester by seven thirty.

LIFE'S RIVER

~ Rivers of tear.
~ Streams of sun.
~ Valleys of despair.
~ Mountains of work.

~ Sea of unrest
~ Fields of glory.
~ Hills to climb.
~ Seeds to sow.

~ Rain in hearts.
~ Icy remarks.
~ Hot air talk.
~ Roses for romance.

~ Starry eyed dreams.
~ Lunar landscapes.
~ Deserts of loneliness.
~ Lakes of wine.

~ All to flow by
~ in one river of life.

One line definition of life experience. There are ingredients in the lines that encapsulate events –not all the time, but perhaps those which can be highlighted as memorable.

SUBLIMINAL TALK

'Marmalade finely cut,
honey in a pot
white and brown bread
~ but only lightly toasted .
Soldiers for the little one.
Cereals for these two.

My husband has a kipper
but sometimes egg and ham.
The silver must be spotless
~ the coffee always with cream.
freshly squeezed orange
must be here upon the table
You need to be aware
that I am the owner's daughter
with the public smiling face.

When my husband opens his paper
hiding his face from view~
~~~ My smile is just for you.

I see you admire
my décolletage
by the look on your well- tanned face.
My request for your later company
is written in perfumed envelope
~ I'm handing now to you.
It would be wise to supply,
for I am the owners' daughter
with the public smiling face.

Your future here will last
only if you ably comply.

That husband over there
is a drone, who benefits
from father owning every stone.'

It's a meeting
I've decided—that
needs to be especially agreeable
Then for me to tell PA that
you're extra-ordinary
—not just plain ordinary in
delivering good silver service.

You have to keep it secret
—between the two of us.
It'll never have happened
When we meet outside my boudoir.
For I am the owner's daughter
with the public smiling face.

~~~~~~~~~~~~~~~~

An imagined possible scenario. Power used
inappropriately in an employer employee relationship.

ESSENCE OF LOVE **MOTHER FIGURE**

You were the one who
      gave time—
to show the way to
      — tie my shoes
direct my hands

winding a tie
feeding it through
— forming a knot .

Who stayed to read.
      Listening patiently, while
I searched for words.
      Bothering the pictures
When I said turn and
-     ~ "You—you tell the story."

But still I did learn—
      How not to
put my elbows on a table.
      To hold a knife
not like a spear but
      in the hand—and
not grasp the spoon
      but place it between
fingers and thumb
      You the adult
I the child
      when no one was there,
save you eldest sister
      who explained to
a little brother
      who wanted a mother.

Elder sisters can be very concerned about the short comings of their young siblings. I was probably better prepared for school than I would otherwise have been.

MILLENNIUM PRIMROSE

The teasel's yet to
grow its prickly cone
above the grass and dandelion.

The ash spreads out
Its branch~ widening
through the years.

The ancient oak
might display, if it could,
a video picture
of changing fashion
in speech and clothes;
as centuries of walkers
pass through.

Pollarded trees
stubbed and muscled
straddle the sky;
before this summer's growth.
Nettles, brambles
~~~~~~ scythed,
free the primrose
to cascade in petal.

Time scurries down a path
for all millennia~ and
in this habitat—the primrose talisman will
advertise every spring.

To break out
Its flower and
captivate all
who seek renewal
beneath the mighty oak.

New generations
will await the arrival
of this early flower.
that greets each
~~~ before leafy branch
takes out
the best of light.

~~~~~~~~~~~~~~~~

> The longevity of trees puts mankind in the shade. The teasel, mentioned at the beginning is still prolific in Frome. Left over from when it was employed to "tease" (brush/straighten the strands) of cloth produced. High quality tailors cloth was produced in Somerset and then sent to London by train.

HOLIDAYS PAST

Victorian buildings,
Mixed with sky
raised tabernacles.
Giant up ended
Match box shapes
Dotted on hills.

Multi-dangling hoops
of lights compete with
Pastiche of Riviera palm.
Forgetting not
garden flowers and greens.

Battered B & B
encoded perhaps with memory
of tourist spilled from train and coach.

To drift along the front
sand in flip flop,
foot and toe.
To stand, sit, beneath palms
when tide takes out the beach.

Fish and chip shop,
Ice cream parlour trade.
Fortunes made at summer end.
Hotels, restaurants, pubs.
With trade aplenty for speedy exit,
at season's close.
To Swiss chalet, heated stove and winter snow.
Ski, après ski, with no return 'til March wind doth blow.

The five deep walk of visitor,
chomping juicy peach.
Caught by never ending rain.

Driven from sandy beach—
into gift and coffee shop.
The cheap plastic macs.
The seaside show that entertained
with song, dance and comic turn

Now a derelict aftermath.
Swapped for foreign holidays, timeshare,
Quick, cheap flights, food and booze.
That once popular playground
For the many, not just a few.

Then, there to be with happy crowds, who
sought reprieve from factory, office toil.
Sitting out in sizzling sun 'til skin
became a lobster pink.

Still to take that chance that clouds, squally rain and
mist will not with them take part.
Living in daily hope, whatever
weather cloak is sent to get
— their taste of heaven.
Those coloured lights that spoke of parties.

Victorian buildings beyond their heyday,
mixed with sky raised tabernacles of today.
The bed and breakfast lodgings.
Choked off, tailed back motorists.
Nose to tail in metallic crocodile queue,
Seeking respite, to bask beside,
Idyllic blue sea, away from fret, fumes and work.

To drift along the front, to catch
The brisk balmy air
And sit beneath the palms.
On cared for gardens and browned in grass.

When waves shut the sandy beach
with whip lash tangy spray.

The fish and chip shops, changing hands,
Fortune's made. The hotels, restaurants, pubs,
bunched with guests enough to
to see owners through,
to their Swiss chalet, heated stove.
To ski, frolic in the snow.
Get skunked in après ski;
with no return 'til March wind blow.

Now all gone in the derelict aftermath,
of foreign holidays, timeshare,
quick cheap flights, bed, food, booze.

The once popular playground
for the Scots, Irish, Welsh
north, south, east west,
and everywhere.

Then to be with happy crowds, who
Sought reprieve from factory,office toil;
to breathe in sunny sea air.
But still to emphasise when
Rain or mist occluded
hope of sunny beach days.

~~~~~~~~~~

An era before Britain discovered foreign holidays and availability of air travel at affordable cost. The relative inexpensiveness of visiting Spain, plus the development of package holidays. These developments really hit the British seaside tourism business hard.

The poem harks back to those days when a good living

66

could be made from running a fish and chip cafe, gift shop, bed and breakfast or even perhaps a hotel serving bed breakfast and evening meal. This during an extended summer season ~April to September. The owners then vacationed to Switzerland or sold up for the winter months. It seems apocryphal, but some business owners achieved this in the halcyon days.

RIDING THROUGH TIME

Can the atrocity of deed
slice time into the ground;
when actuality is caught,
to be seen again, again.

An army nearly slaughtered,
seen by horror stricken few;
now terror prints indelibly,
the place for evermore.

They raced away from carnage
on battle weary horse;
across a field of corn;
then scythed to death by sword.

Now the night is still;
new generation fast asleep.
A band of ghostly horseman,
chase the field once more.

      Note Reference: There is mention, in Leicestershire, of a band of ghostly horseman seen crossing fields in moonlight. They are dressed in Royalist uniform with feathered hats long boots, buckles and swords. There was a group of horseman, who were caught by Cromwell's army and all slaughtered. This was in 1645, following the defeat of Charles the First's army at the Battle of Naseby.
      Destined, perhaps, to reappear, now in ghostly form, down the centuries.

SHE LEFT...

I loved her very much;
till we had a batch.
She took the cat.
It wasn't a match.

I miss the cat more;
but not her Chihuahua.

Her absence not
the loss it should have been.

It was deceit to believe,
she'd stay when
earning thrice more
than me.

She prosecuted her case
from false evidence.
I never even got a kiss, in later days.
Let alone supposed extra love affair.

Another fatal female,
who earned thrice more.
Broadcasting charm,
to advance career.

Here I stand upon the sand.
Well more in a band,
caught up with others.
At her beck and call.

Not about work,
but wanting to be
in Lara's life.
Not just being sliced.

Not a part only spare;
left by one, not heart broken,
But this one doesn't even really care.
Let alone permit an affair.

~~~~~~~~~~~~~~~~

> The poem is James's lament and relates to his break up with Nina, in the novel and the seemingly unattainable distance that exists between him and the possibility of a relationship with Lara—his boss.

LOVE- STARVED BY ELECTRONICS

D' you not mind that we no longer meet?
over lingered coffee in a café corner.
That we are now in distant town and place.
In each quirky message I see your smile.
Both day and night I feel despair and loss.
Survival dependant on your next new message.
Reply, reply, for I do just hold to life.
Write of our future, not of summers past.
You and me sharing every waking moment.
Life's, purpose, meaning lost 'til your return.

Sleep denies me through the night watches;
for I hope even then for possible new message;
while simply starved of your real presence;
Real voice, smile and face- not all electronic.

~~~~~~~~~~~~~~~~~~~~

This was selected in a competition for an anthology. The theme was—Sonnets for Shakespeare.

SPIRIT OF SPRING

It has to be the daffodils
which bravely sprout
from mother earth,
stung cold from
Arctic wind.
In shortened days,
of ice and snow.

How dare they dance
These ballerina's so
in delicate attire to
question winter's blast?

How foolish, perhaps
their belief, purpose, reason
to enthral our sight,
with rhapsodic dance?
When such a force,
That stripped the leaves
from mighty oak
inhabits still the cold dark earth.

Yet, Perhaps their triumph
Is more than just defiance.
Heralds of communication
beyond our eyes and ears,
transmitting to
dormant realms
good news of
return toward the flow of warmth and light.

A flower to greet,
applaud rebirth.
Vibrant early

colour in this forbidding world.
Primary brush strokes.
Scene setting for the approach
of Nature's master class.

The poem was selected for an anthology about the seasons.

THE PLANTED COPSE

A path steepens its weave thru' the copse.
Planted inhabitants reach high the sky,
yet not excluding every light.
Bare spokes of lifeless branch
give perch for squirrel, bird.

Young trees with needle clumps
sticky mark the hand.
Old giants with black silvered bark,
display seep of resin; amber coloured-
like frozen trickled blood;,
from way inside a heart.

Sinuous limbs threaded first in ground,
now push up on red earthed paths.
Bleached brown needles of seasons past,
make soft the ground to tread.

All that's heard is
The pine canopy catching
releasing the breeze
beneath the clouds.

Earlier messaging
to this onlooker pictures
of waves breaking
on a sunlit beach.
    Now breath-like sighs
to match the weakened pulse
of a broken heart.

The romance ended. The poem seeks to capture the moment of return to the copse. The trees were witness to the previous happy event. The continuity of life is such that the pine trees will still be there –The pine canopy catching and

> Releasing the breeze
> Beneath the clouds.

THANKFUL THOUGHTS

The hands, activity of minds;
    building highways,
reservoirs, digital communications;
    that which we readily
accept day to day;
    not always giving thanks.

To provide menu for living;
    for man, woman, child.
That often
    takes for granted
the action of the many;
    preparing, providing
from daily toil;
    heat, light, water;
material ingredient of life.

To provide for now and
    future life
in the cycle
    of forming birth.
To understand that it's
    the work of many;
all equal in regard
    for one Perpetual Mind.
Thankfulness be given,
    determinedly in all ages
to all true presence
    of care and understanding
to quiet the troubled mind.

It is a theme that implies the existence of the Creator, but also, recognition that, human hands, minds and hearts strive to build, repair and maintain the structure of our material existence. The growing of crops, animal husbandry, water workers, road builders, transport workforces~ over land sea and air~ and the oil industry, which has transformed our lives by providing ready energy from oil exploration and discovery. There are so many work forces, which contribute to our day to day existence— all of these mentioned and many more besides deserve our prayers and thanksgiving.

THAT FIRST MEETING

We met in written letter.
Then in photos sent.
You at some party,
face framed
In feather boa.
I asked for perfume;
You added this
In the next letter.

    Neat written pages
immersed in scent;
were an aphrodisiac
that complemented
attentive, but perhaps
inventive letters.

We made a decision
For us to meet
after that first
romance of letters.

A picture jigsaw,
made in our minds.
We wanted then
to arrange a
meeting in 3D.

'It's me,' you said
on the station platform.
I'd looked and looked away;
not sure you were the photo girl.
Perhaps, you saw me clearly
from the letters written.
' Hello,' in a quiet voice, I said.

My lack of recognition not
that upsetting. After all
No photo captures everything.

In a slim hand
you held a car key.
'At last we've met'—you said.
'The car's outside.'
~ We must have talked,
when we left.

From the passenger seat
I noticed, trembling of your legs and
feet when they moved on
accelerator and clutch.
~ It was a nervous first meeting,
for the both of us.

You looked across and smiled
~ asked about the journey.
It was a good beginning.

We became engaged,
for a little while;
but, in fairness, only
one of us did love.
You already had another,
who awaited your return.

The relationship depicted in the poem was from
long distant letter writing. It went the full course to
engagement. You probably need to later tell yourself that
marriage would never have worked. That it was probably
realistic for it to end. Not an easy call to make.

A SHORELINE OF LOVE

Tantalizing, captivating,
that smile transmitting
across the sand exclusively
from you to me.
The psychedelic bikini-
- vivid green and blue.
Your slim fingers on knees
eyes turned to me;
biting deep
with mischievous intent;
deftly positioned
pink scarf;

concealing those
marked kisses.
But you let
the breeze to catch
your hair.
The sun a hand maiden
danced attendance,
in your presence.

A recall
carved in time.
Contented smile,
soothing, bathing, inwardly caressing.
Forever caught in the swirl,
that spills and fills,
through and through;
of love caught
in one moment.
We parted;
but memory's fresh.

Of rainbow texture;
wakening the mind to break on
a shoreline of love.

~~~~~~~~~~~~~~~~~~~~

Relationships of note—stored away, but bubbling to life when triggered by some experience in everyday life. A colour, musical note, someone's wave, a smile, the trill of bird song, a gentle breeze across the face. No real understanding of why or how, but taken in the moment. The moment that is— now the present.

WINTER RIVER RACE

Cords knitted thru' many eyelets,
strung tight by days of damp;
nails picking, taut knots,
remembering
from last week's episodic race.

The cold canvas cover's like cardboard:
removal releases stench;
from the wet evaporation
of the muddied salt river.

Sagging buoyancy bags;
now re- blown from lips, with
lungs catching draughts of,
~ cold morning air.

A twist of cold stung shackle pin,
punishes finger and thumb.
Unstitching sausage shaped sail bag,
reaching for mainsail, and jib.

Clipping main to boom;
feeding sail past chilled hands;
pushing battens in scabbard like openings.
Fastening jib with pinched open clips.

Forming figure of eight knot,
preventing sheet's escape.
Not then forgetting,
cork drainage plugs to put in.

Trundling the boat on trolley,
to muddy rock, green weed river.
Wind suddenly, grasping, shaking,
rigging, - mainsail and jib.

Feet, calves stunned;
by water's close cousin to ice.
Finger's flex and grip to
escape full capture by cold.

The crinkly rattle of sail,
caught in boisterous wind.
A final push of foot,
on pebbled river bed.

A prising in of rudder;
attaching of the tiller.
Ready to weave 'cross river.
To race, perhaps to win.

~~~~~~~~~~~~

> The river experienced tidal flow and stank handsomely when the tide was low. It still maintained a commanding presence with a briny stench mix of mud and weed, even with the tide in. The river Teign was my first long acquaintance with a river. Sunday race meets on the River Teign.

THE G THREE SUMMIT

- 'You are called to be
acquainted with the
difficulty of being~ authenticated,'
said Red~ it was always Red who
opened the Summit.

' We do not "exist" save
when regulated, approved and collated.
How disgusting is that?'

'No interruptions,~ a late arrival
Violet blue lit up, but
dimmed when told to by Red.

'I speak for Blue and Yellow.'
They were given no choice
Although the talk was about Green
' We are ill-used in process.
Abstracted from ourselves.

'I'm rarely shown as
vibrant, but dark
and uninteresting on film.
In magma~ light
floods to blue
and even Yellow can intrude!'
~ Red bitterly complained.

' I expect to be portrayed
in an honesty
that displays my
mesmerising presence,
~ that is all I ask.'

'We meet, we three

to be true to ourselves.
No longer maligned
by camera lens
YOU- gathered around us
are only derivatives-
out of our primary being,
splintered away by dilution.'

'This summit is called
to let you see
that our perfection
remains- indisputable.'

'Green has been given
a position nearer to us-only
While Spring leads to Summer.'

'I, recognize in Green an
ability to dress the natural order
of plant, tree, fern, grass, and- even moss.
We applaud this enhancement.'
-Red assumed a regal
status above all others.

' Yellow and Blue, anything to add?'
They were supportive,
since Green was for them
a product of a kind of marriage.

Blue held back but Yellow
answered with a timid -'no.'
Both found Red extremely daunting.

-'Then it's decided
to allow Green- slight elevation—
Green's value's recognized
to complement our

multi- colour show,
thru' summer.
But I reserve the
right to include
Purple and Orange
~for especial effect,
notwithstanding
this late day decision.

~~~~~~~~~~~~~~~~~~

Typically animals are the voice of a fable. I liked the idea of colours, even plants with voices. The G Summits attract the world media. The leaders of powerful nations congregate to discuss matters of world importance. This is a summit for three dominant colours. Red is a powerful and dominant colour. It seemed right that red should have all the swagger and sway. There is an element of insecurity for all the bombast.
    Big personalities invariably want to be liked for all their outspokenness and showiness. Red, senses that on his or her own there may be times when a mix~ with yellow, blue and black may be required to find selection by the artist. Red does have insecurities!

POEM: ABOUT WINTER

Ice upon the pond
Digs deep all winter long.
Pond lily leaves in aspic.

The ground frost,
bites, even on bare branch
denying colour~ access.

Sun but partially blinks
to stare on frost and ice.
Before black again the night.

Blank canvas portrayed for days
with total carpet spread
where even daylight
seems short of breath.

Nature hibernates
Beneath the icy ground.
Colds persistence
forces us inside.
Minds stoked perhaps with imaginings
of summers past and yet to come.

Time to pause, reflect.
To work on that near forgotten project.
We enjoy the glow of Summer,
But not for ever and a day.
winter gives appreciation

for family, hearth and home.
Adventures still abounding
but now more of the mind.
Grateful in time to reflect on
memory and experience gained.

A space to prepare for the
new year that lies ahead.

~~~~~~~~~~~~~~~~

It is the understanding that winter is a passing phase. It maybe long, but the sun returns to warm the earth. The state of mind within us need not be dark. The trees have taken a selected departure from their dress and dance in the wind. The roots can still respond to the warmth from the air above, when spring arrives to re-supply growth.

We also can repair our approach to life. To be perhaps more understanding of others. Prepared to strike out with our new growth, and be forgiving and more in tune with others.

INSTANT COFFEE MAKING

Start a kettle's journey to the boil.
    Requisition teaspoon, cup, mug,
ruler, coffee in a jar.
        If not a purist, milk and sugar too.
    Add with teaspoon coffee, powder, granules
        both distant from their instant claim~
until the water boils. One teaspoon or
    two to smack alive a vegetated state.
The kettle will not boil,
    in human time,
so make out you care not.
    Stare at flowers,
stroke the cat;
    write a poem,
don't give a drat.
    Then when it clicks
be nonchalant~ make it wait
    some seconds too.
Lift kettle, pour into mug, savour~
    ~ aroma -get the full deal.
If you prefer white, not black
    measure with ruler three centimetre gap,
from lip of mug a space for milk. Then add.
    Sugar addiction remember needs
that teaspoon stir.

In a group setting we were asked to write about making coffee. A twenty minute exercise.

THE TIME MAKER'S KINGDOM

Time it swirls,
unwinds and curls
across this dimension.

No! I cannot take
you there just yet.
But if you promise
not to tell your
closest friend
or anyone at all
I will time's secret
storage place reveal.

You must agree
and say after me.
"Reveal the mystery now."

Good.

This is the chant
that unlocks the
memory vault
to reveal
where time
hides all event.

I hear the ethereal
dancing spin
from nearby
asteroid and comet;
while a part of me
stands to view
next door to time,
a totality of all
captured within

its multi- cabled layers.

This being twisting
seamlessly to its never
ending destination.

When asked for an epoch
It gives an age.
Then it narrows down, down
through millennium
to year thousands,
which are but an epoch
tick of millisecond.

Century, decade, year,
day, month, hour, minute and
millionth of a second.
Time will produce
"that" which was once,
just once— a now.

The now brought back to
here, whenever the
appropriate request
is made.

All that's ever been
exists within times
swirling tunnel.

Enter, at
a point and it will answer
your request to be in that
place
~~~~~ to live and breathe
from memory believed
now spent.

the past to see again;
This many faceted coiled
file record of all that's ever been.

Forever known, forever there~ for
recall in the Time Maker's Kingdom.

A children's poem. Poems can often only come fully alive when read or recited from memory. In songs there can be a refrain for the audience to join in with. The attempt here is to catch interest early on. The poem asks the listener to contribute. The listener is drawn in and the secret unfolds and is revealed Or is it?

CODED IN THE WIND

A cool breeze will speak to you,
but you may not listen.
It can flow across your face
and lips—with tingled
sense~ like after rapid speech.

Yet you've not spoken. Only felt and heard
the rise and fall from this enchantress
that inhabits earthly region

A presence that insists itself
into your life
with need to both talk and hear
About more and more.
An invitation sent to each
man, woman, bird, animal.
To catch notes that ripple through
leaves from this multi fingered harpist.
Then print rec-cord on invisible membrane;
bars, splodged notes, but authentic, individual
~music within each life.
Breeze swirl in and out of portals
~ forever entering, departing, entering,
departing~ never requesting;
in ways that may cool,
refresh, heat strewn lands~
~unleash storm crescendo.
Then spectacularly arrive
to shake, shudder, stall
man's tedious arrogance.
~~~ Spread terror to living creatures
Its howl-like scream
feeds ferocious gusts, rip cord storms.

A violent form in cloaked visibility;
but in fearsome awesome presence.

Still to ripple through leaves
like many fingers across harp strings.
Its cold blast companionship
when you are clothed, healthy and fed;
strong in breath and limb;
to stride with strength
'cross moorland, hill, beach,
meadow, lamp lit street.

ANCESTRAL SAVANNAH

(Early human habitat was "Savannah"
not forest~Scientists continue to argue
~The decision has been made by this poet)

Thoughts beat through my mind
of those Savannah plains,
where we foraged far and wide
and returned with food.

For fit, strong, weak, sick
young, old:

~ Our tribe.

Remember:
pestilence, famine, drought.
Those mauled
when hunting
on the plain.

Remember:
also the wisdom of elders
whose tenacious minds
could advise and recall
seasons past.
Forever, able
to make light of troubles:
~rearm our strength

Remember:
on those gateway plains
darting in and out
to hide in
grass our height;
from those who
knew us as their prey.

Savanah, birthplace, which
gave food, breath and life.
but could be~ with anguish countered.
Remember: minds and bodies
in weakened state~
that made show of fear.

Remember how the gods rescued us from out the darkness
~~with new light; once more to give
song, dance~ to sooth our troubled state..
Build resolve, hope and joy
on that Savannah Homeland.